Coming to a Place of Abiding

Equipping believers to come to a place of abiding by appropriating the present ministry of Jesus in the heavenly realms through the prayers of Yahweh.

by Clyde J Hodson

COMING TO A PLACE OF ABIDING

All scripture quotations are taken from the Holy Bible: New International Version (NIV)

ISBN -13: 978-1720365495
ISBN-10: 1720365490

I want to thank Becky Scheffrahn, Jeanine Smith, and Carolyn Trimmer for reading through this material and giving very valuable input to its final product. To Carol Harris for her work in the coordination and editing of this publication. Special thanks are in order to Jack Jackson, Beth Marshall, and Larry Yandell for encouragement and contribution to the editing and proofing of this booklet. I am grateful to my wife, Mary Lynne and daughters, Kara, Lindsay and Meagan who have patiently allowed me to seek the Lord in prayer in the early hours of the morning and come to a place of abiding in Him.

For more information about this ministry, please contact:

*Prayer*Mentor
Clyde Hodson
PO Box 13856
Arlington, TX 76094
www.prayermentor.org
clydehodson@prayermentor.org

Table of Contents

YAHWEH PRAYER GUIDE

This prayer guide identifies various situations believers and their loved ones may encounter and recommends the Yahweh prayers that address each situation:

Fallen Away

Growing

Guilt/Shame

Hard Times

Healing

Protection

Provision

Introduction

Jesus prayed.

As Jesus was baptized He prayed and heaven opened up, the Spirit came upon Him like a dove and the Father affirmed Him as the Son. Luke 3:21,22

The Spirit led Jesus into the wilderness to be tempted by the devil. Jesus fasted for forty days and when the devil challenged His role as the Son, He resisted the devil with the Word of God. Jesus returned to Galilee in the power of the Holy Spirit and began in ministry. Luke 4:1-15

When faced with the seduction of success in Capernaum as the whole town came to Him, Jesus rose early in the morning while it was still dark and went to a solitary place to pray. Peter found Jesus later that morning and exclaimed: "Everyone is looking for You". Jesus told him that He had to go to other villages to preach, for that is what He was sent to do. Mark 1:32-39; Luke 4:42-44

Though the news about Jesus spread, so that crowds of people came to hear Him and to be healed of their sicknesses, He often withdrew to lonely places and prayed. Luke 5:15, 16

Sometime after Jesus had called His disciples to follow Him and promised to make them fishers of men, He went to the mountainside to pray. He spent the night praying to God. The next morning He called His disciples to Himself. He chose the twelve and appointed them as apostles. Luke 6:12-16

After Jesus fed the five thousand, He resisted the seduction of being made king and withdrew to the mountain where He prayed into the night. Jesus walked on water later that night. The next day He declared that He was the bread of life. He was not offering a physical kingdom where they would be fed, but rather a spiritual kingdom and eternal life. When the multitudes could not accept His words and left Him, the twelve remained with Jesus because He had the words of life. Matt 14:13-33; Jn 6

Jesus prayed and then He asked His disciples, "Who do men say that I am?" Through Jesus' prayers, Peter was given revelation to declare that Jesus was the Christ, the Son of the Living God. Jesus then told His disciples that upon the rock of Peter's confession He would build His church. Jesus also disclosed that He would go to Jerusalem and suffer at the hands of the religious leaders and be put to death. Luke 9:18-22

Nine days later Jesus prayed and Peter, James and John beheld His glory on the mount of transfiguration. Luke 9:29

Jesus prayed and His disciples asked Him to teach them to pray. Jesus repeated the instruction He gave concerning prayer from the Sermon on the Mount. Along with this instruction, Jesus taught them a parable of the persistent neighbor. Jesus wanted His disciples to understand that answered prayer comes out of the desperation of seeing a need realizing their lack of resources to meet the need and bold persistence in prayer to the One who has the resources to meet the need. Luke 11:1-13

Satan desired to sift Peter as wheat, but Jesus prayed for him that his faith would not fail, and it didn't. Jesus protected His disciples in prayer by the name the Father gave Him. Luke 22:31,32

Jesus prayed often in the garden of Gethsemane with His disciples. On the night He was betrayed, Jesus prayed while His disciples slept. When Judas and the soldiers came to arrest Him, Jesus did not respond with violence nor did He run away. Jesus found the strength to bear the cup of wrath the Father had for Him and be the atonement for the sins of the world because He prayed. Luke 22:39-46

In His death, Jesus was numbered with the transgressors and He made intercession for them. Is. 53:12

Now, as the ascended Lord, Jesus is a High Priest after the order of Melchizedek and He lives forever to make intercession for the saints. Heb 7:24,25

Throughout His ministry, Jesus prayed. In His death, Jesus prayed. Now, being seated at the right hand of the Father, Jesus is praying.

Why did Jesus pray? What moved the Son of God to seek the Father's face and pray? Jesus prayed for three reasons:

1. As God the Son, Jesus loved the Father and sought oneness with Him in prayer in that He might know and obey the Father's will,

2. As God the Son, Jesus advanced the Kingdom by force, taking ground away from the prince of this world and the powers of darkness through prayer,

3. As God the Son, Jesus revealed the Father to His disciples and gave them the words the Father gave Him as a result of prayer.

The first reason of loving the Father and seeking oneness with Him in prayer is the focus of this booklet. The purpose of this booklet is to assist and encourage believers to come to a place of abiding in Christ in the heavenly realms by appropriating the present ministry of Jesus as they pray through the names of Yahweh. This place of abiding positions them with the authority of Christ, so that their prayers may be answered.

A little less than a hundred years ago, a young Welsh coal miner named Reese Howells gave himself to intercession on behalf of the lost. Mr. Howells was a part of the Welsh Revivals early in the twentieth century. Every night of the week Howells led meetings and called chapels for a group of seekers. In his walks to and from the chapels, he spent time in prayer. Howells spoke of a place of abiding where he waited upon God daily during the time in which the intercession lasted. He prayed day after day until a new position of intercession was gained. That position of intercession was a place of spiritual authority in prayer [1].

Since 1989 I have been praying through the Lord's Prayer regularly. My introduction to praying through the Lord's Prayer as a daily discipline came as I read Larry Lea's book, Could You Not Tarry For One Hour. During these times of meditation and intercession, while praying through the Lord's Prayer, the Spirit taught me deep truths about the person and work of Christ. What I discovered is that Jesus is alive! He is waiting for me to draw near to Him, enter into a relationship with Him, and take hold of all the resources of His present ministry. It is in the process of praying through the names of Yahweh, in affirming the truth of Scripture, listening for His voice and responding to Him that enables me to enter a place of abiding. It is in this place that I find the presence and power of Christ working in me and through me for His glory. It is in this place that I am connected to the Head of the Church and listen for His mind. As a result, I have found an anointing and authority to fulfill my calling and advance the Kingdom of God through prayer.

For many believers prayer is an illusive idea. It is difficult to get our arms around the notion of being still and talking to God. We suppose that prayer is passive in nature, so we see it as an empty practice of talking into the air. Receiving answers to our prayers from God seems even more illusive. We hear others give testimony of their heavenly Father meeting with them, giving them direction in prayer and answering their prayers. Yet, that is not our experience. But wait, there is good news for us all!

Jesus invites all of His followers to abide in Him.[2] When Jesus speaks of abiding, He is using the word picture of a branch remaining in the vine to illustrate the oneness that is available to His followers. His desire is that believers would experience the same kind of oneness with Him that He experienced with His heavenly Father. In His pursuit of oneness with the Father, Jesus prayed. Just as the Father revealed Himself to the Son, lived in Him and did His work through Him (John 14:10), so the Lord Jesus desires to reveal Himself to His followers, live His life within them and do His work through them. Jesus promised His followers the very same kind of oneness He experienced with His Father (John 14:20).

Jesus promised that if we abide in Him and His word abides in us, we can ask whatever we wish and He will give us our request. What an amazing promise! There is no limit to Jesus' promise for answered prayer in this statement to His disciples. The key to the fulfillment of His promise is in the condition of abiding.[3] Abiding brings a whole new dimension to the nature of prayer. So what was Jesus talking about when He invited His disciples to abide in Him?

Jesus surprised His disciples three times as they shared their last Passover meal together. Jesus' first surprise was to wash the disciples feet. He had heard His followers arguing with one another about who would be first in the Kingdom. Aware that no one had washed their feet, Jesus took hold of a teachable moment and taught them a lesson on servanthood by washing their feet. Jesus surprised His followers a second time when He disclosed that one of them was going to betray Him. On the heels of that announcement, Jesus surprised the disciples a third time when He said He was going away to prepare a place for them. He promised that He will come back to them and that He will receive them to Himself so that they may be where He is. In this regard, He promised to ask the Father to send another Counselor like Himself to live within them. He talked about how their love relationship with Him was expressed in keeping His commands. Jesus promised that He would disclose Himself to them. Jesus' intention was to communicate that they would experience a spiritual oneness with Him; in the same way He and the Father were one.

The meal completed, they sang a hymn and began their walk to the Garden of Gethsemane where they would pray. On the way, Jesus taught an object lesson about the oneness they would experience with Him, using the vine and the branches. Jesus invited His disciples to abide in Him. It is as though He was saying, "Everything I have been talking about in the last portion of our meal together is illustrated in this vine and branches. I am inviting you to experience a oneness with me, even though I will be gone."

There are four questions that are essential to understanding what Jesus is talking about when He invites His disciples to abide in Him:

1.   Why do we abide in Christ?

2.   Where is this place of abiding?

17

3.   What does it mean to abide in Christ?

4.   How do we abide in Christ?

In answering these questions, an entirely new perspective is given to help believers understand Jesus' invitation to abide in Him.

Why do we abide in Christ?

Jesus made three conditional promises for those followers who will abide in Him. Jesus promised that if His disciples abide in Him:

1.   He (Jesus) will abide in them,

2.   They will bear much fruit, and

3.   They will have answered prayer.

Jesus then defines the purpose of abiding. Abiding brings glory to the Father.

Why does a follower of Christ abide in Jesus? It is as the believer abides in Jesus that He lives His life in and through him. It is as the believer abides in Christ that he bears much fruit for the Father's glory. Finally it is as the believer abides in Christ that his prayers are answered.

Where is this place of abiding?

The answer to that question is found in another question, where is Jesus right now?

1.   Jesus is at the right hand of the Father in the heavenly realms, and

2.   Jesus is living within the hearts of His followers.

First, As believers abide in Christ they are seated with Him in the heavenly realms as members of His body at the right hand of the Father. After Jesus reveals to His followers that one of them is going to betray Him, He encourages them not to let their hearts be troubled. Jesus promises that His Father's house had many dwelling places. He says that He was going away to prepare a place for them. He then promises that He will return and receive them to Himself. I want to suggest that when Jesus says He is going away to prepare a place, He is referring to His work of redemption on the cross. When He promises that He will return to them, He is referring to the resurrection. When He promises that He will receive them to Himself, He is referring to Pentecost when the Spirit is poured out and baptizes His followers into His body, (1Cor 12:13) so that they may be where Jesus is. So where is Jesus? Jesus is seated at the right hand of the Father in the heavenly realms. Jesus has a position of authority above all the heavenly beings. He is the head of the church, which is His body. In God's great love and mercy He has made all those who are followers of Jesus alive. He raised them and seated them with Jesus in the heavenly realms. Believers are members of the body of Christ seated with Jesus, their Head.

Second, Jesus promises that He and the Father will make their dwelling within those who love Him and keep His commands, (John 14:2). Jesus promises that if His followers abide in Him, He will abide in them. Where is Jesus? He is living within every believer through the third person of the trinity, the Spirit of Truth. The apostle Paul affirmed this truth to the Corinthian believers when he says. "We have this treasure in jars of clay to show that this all surpassing power is from God and not from us." (2Cor 4:7)   Paul affirms the life of Jesus living within him when he says, "We always carry around in our body the death of Jesus, so that the life of Jesus may also be revealed in our body." (2Cor 4:10) Jesus promises that He is going to live His life in the believer. Later as Jesus dialogues with His followers in His last supper with them, He promises, "In that day, you will know that I am in the Father, you are in me and I am in you." John 14:20 I want to suggest that when Jesus says, "You are in Me" He is referring to the believer being seated with Him as members of His body in the heavenly realms at the right hand of the Father. When Jesus says, "I am in you" He is referring to Himself being the treasure within the earthen vessel, His follower.

Therefore, the place of abiding for believers is:

1.   Being seated with Christ, the head of the church, as members of His body at the right hand of the Father,

2.   Wherever believers are in this life, because Jesus is abiding in them and makes His home in them.

What does it mean to abide in Christ?

The life of Abiding in Christ is based on what the believer does and what Jesus does. First, Jesus told His disciples, "If you love me, you will keep my commands." Jesus, the Jewish Rabbi, said it three times, (John 14:15, 21, 23) emphasizing that love and obedience is the most important thing they can do in their relationship with Him. Jesus calls His followers to love Him and this love is expressed through obedience to His commands. This is the very kind of relationship Jesus had with the Father. Towards the end of His discussion with the disciples, at the Passover meal, Jesus speaks of the prince of this world coming to try and hinder Him from obeying the Father and going to the cross. Jesus asserts that the devil has nothing on Him, but that He loves the Father and does exactly what His Father commands Him. The same relationship Jesus had with the Father, one of love and obedience, is the relationship He is calling His followers to have with Him.

Second, Jesus promised an intimacy and oneness with His followers. After each of the three conditional statements of love and obedience in John 14, Jesus promises that He would reveal Himself to them:

1.   "Before long, the world will not see Me anymore, but you will see Me (John 14:19)."

2.   "He who loves Me will be loved by My Father, and I too will love him and show Myself to him (John 14:21)."

3.   "My Father will love him, and We will come to him and make Our home with him (John 14:23)."

Jesus speaks of the very same kind of intimacy and oneness He experiences with the Father. He says, "On that day you will realize that I am in My Father, and you are in Me, and I am in you." This is what Jesus means when He later said if they will abide in Him, He will abide in them. Jesus desires to live His life in and through His followers. This is the very kind of relationship Jesus has with the Father. Jesus says, "If you really knew Me, you would know My Father as well. From now on, you do know Him and have seen Him." (John 14:7) Again Jesus says, "Anyone who has seen Me has seen the Father...Don't you believe that I am in the Father, and that the Father is in Me? The words I say to you are not just My own. Rather, it is the Father, living in Me, who is doing His work. Believe Me when I say that I am in the Father and the Father is in Me; or at least believe on the evidence of the miracles themselves."(John 14:9-11) Just as the Father was living in Jesus and doing His work in Him, Jesus desires to live His life in His followers and do His work through them.

Therefore, to abide in Christ is, first and foremost, a love relationship with Jesus, being seated with Him in the heavenly realms. This love is expressed through obedience to His commands as the Head of the body. Second, to abide in Christ is to experience intimacy and oneness with Jesus as He lives His life in and through His followers.

How do we abide in Christ?

We abide in Christ through the ministry of the Holy Spirit. I had been praying through Larry Lea's outline of the Lord's Prayer for fifteen months and I have to admit at times it got old. The spring of water that refreshes and gives life to my soul after the first year was drying up. As I was awakened one morning by my alarm, a praise song was on my heart. I thought, "That is a great song, but I have to go pray." As I was waiting for the coffee to drip into the mug, the same song came to mind. Again I thought, "Awesome song, but I have to go pray." Two hundred yards into my prayer walk that song once again came to mind. This time I thought, "I need to sing this song." I began singing with all my heart and immediately I was in the presence of God worshipping. The Spirit gave me that song and my prayer time was all together different as I yielded to the Spirit's leading. The spiritual intimacy and oneness that Jesus is speaking of can only be experienced by the ministry of the Holy Spirit[1]. Jesus repeatedly promised another Counselor during that last evening with His disciples. Jesus asked the Father to send the Holy Spirit to them. It is by the ministry of the Counselor, the Spirit of Truth, that Jesus makes Himself known to believers. Jesus promises that the Spirit will:

1. be in His followers,

2. teach them all things,

3. remind His followers of everything He said to them,

4. testify about Him,

5. convict the world of guilt,

6. guide His followers into all truth,

7. tell them what is yet to come, and

8. bring glory to Jesus by taking from what is His and making it known to them.

Later that evening as Jesus prays His priestly prayer recorded in John 17, He expresses His desire, "Father, I want those You have given to Me to be with Me where I am, and to see My glory." The apostle Paul prays two prayers within his letter to the Ephesian church, asking for the ministry of the Holy Spirit in the lives of those believers.

In the first prayer, Paul is asking for the ministry of the Spirit to give believers wisdom and revelation to know God better. It is the Spirit who gives wisdom to know who God is. It is the Spirit who gives revelation, encounters with the God of the Bible. He prays a second request and asks the Father to enlighten the eyes of their hearts to know the hope to which He has called them, the riches of His glorious inheritance in the saints and His incomparably great power for those who believe. It is the Spirit who gives us an understanding to know the spiritual realities that are ours in the heavenly realms in Christ. In essence, the apostle is asking the Father in the first request to give them encounters with Christ so that they may know Him by experience and in the second request to make their position, being seated with Christ in the heavenly places, a reality in their lives.

In the second prayer the apostle prays for the ministry of the Holy Spirit to strengthen the Ephesian believers with power in the inner person so that Christ may dwell in their hearts by faith. He makes a second request that they may have power to understand the height, width, breadth and depth of the love of Christ and to know by experience His love. In essence Paul is asking the Father in the first request to make the presence of Christ a reality in their hearts and in the second request to give them the ability to experience of the love of Christ as a reality. Paul is praying for both realms of the place of abiding, being seated with Jesus in the heavenly realms and Jesus living within the follower of Christ to be a reality . In these prayers he is asking for the Spirit to fulfill the desire Jesus expressed to the Father as he prays, "Father, I want those...to be with Me where I am." (John 17:24)

So how do believers come to a place of abiding in a practical way? This process of coming to a place of abiding is a matter of both the Spirit and the heart. Coming to a place of abiding is more than going through a prayer list or an outline of prayer. It is a spiritual reality that can only be entered into when it is facilitated by the ministry of the Holy Spirit in believers hearts. It is as believers practice the spiritual disciplines of the Word, worship, solitude and prayer in dependence upon the Spirit of God that believers can experience an encounter with the living Lord Jesus Christ and be in that place of oneness/abiding in Him. Through the spiritual discipline of the Word, the Spirit of Truth reveals truth to believers from God's Word (1Cor. 2:10) concerning the person and work of Jesus and they affirm that truth in their hearts and in the heavenlies. Through the spiritual discipline of worship, the Holy Spirit gives believers a song of praise and/or thanksgiving (John 4:24), and they exalt the One who sits on the throne and express their gratitude to Him. Through the spiritual discipline of solitude (Luke 4:1, 2, 42), the Counselor quiets their hearts and reveals the soft, gentle voice of the Lord Jesus. Through the spiritual discipline of prayer, the Spirit leads believers in their intercession (Eph. 6:18), and they stand in the gap on behalf of others in the heavenly realms. If their prayers are not led and empowered by the Holy Spirit, they are merely going through the motions.

Coming to a place of abiding is more than an intellectual exercise. It is an encounter with the living Christ from the heart. Throughout the Old Testament there are repeated exhortations for the children of Israel to respond to God with all their hearts.

1. Seek the Lord with all your heart – God's people are exhorted to seek the Lord their God with all their heart (Deut. 4:29). The whole point of prayer is to pursue the face of the living Christ with all that is within them. The promise of Scripture is that they will find the Son and come to that place of abiding/oneness, if they look for Him with all of their hearts (Matt. 7:7,8).

2. Love the Lord with all your heart – God's people are repeatedly exhorted to love the Lord with all their heart (Deut. 6:5). John records in the book of Revelation the words of Jesus to the church in Ephesus where He exhorts them to return to their first love. In John 14, Jesus calls His disciples to abide in His love (John 15:9). In this love relationship, believers give their affection to God rather than the things of the world (1John 2:15-17). This love relationship is characterized by an emotional openness with Jesus where believers are honest about their desires, disappointments, fears, grief, hopes, joys, resentments, shame and triumphs (John 8:32). Loving Jesus with all their heart involves surrendering to the lover of their soul, their hopes, dreams, plans, rights and choices (Rom. 12:1,2; 6:13).

3. Obey the Lord with all your heart – God's people are repeatedly exhorted to give all that is within them to carefully observe the

commands of the Lord (Deut. 26:16,17). Again, Jesus repeatedly said if His followers love Him they would keep His commands. Within the process of coming to a place of abiding, believers invite the Holy Spirit to search their hearts (Ps. 139:23,24) and to convict them of their sins (John 16:8). They wait for the Spirit to restore them to a place of rightness and relationship with Jesus. (1John 1:9). They then present themselves as instruments of righteousness to Jesus anew (Rom. 6:13).

4. <u>Trust the Lord with all your heart</u> – God's people are exhorted to trust in the Lord and not lean on their own understanding (Prov. 3:5,6). Although the normative experience of believers is to know by experience the presence of Jesus and the reality of being seated with Him in the heavenly realms (Eph. 2:6), there are times when these realities can only be affirmed by faith. Believers affirm by faith the Biblical truth about Jesus and the spiritual realities of the presence of Christ living within them (Gal. 2:20). Believers rest in the goodness and justice of God for answered prayer regardless of their feelings (Matt. 7:9-11; Luke 18:7,8).

5. <u>Serve the Lord with all your heart</u> – God's people are repeatedly exhorted to serve the Lord with all their heart (Deut. 10:12). Coming to the place of abiding/oneness enables believers to serve the Lord Jesus. In that place, as members of the body of Christ, they are listening for the mind of their Head that they might please Him in all that they do (John 8:28, 29). The very purpose of coming to the place of abiding is that Jesus, as the Vine, may live His life in and through believers, and that they, as the branches, might bear much fruit to the Father's glory. (John 15:5).

To do anything less than to give their whole heart to Jesus is to miss the kind of oneness/intimacy Jesus is inviting His disciples to experience with Him in John 14 & 15.

When Jesus taught His disciples to pray in the sermon on the mount, He gave them an outline known as the Lord's Prayer. I want to suggest the Lord's Prayer was intended to be a focus of prayer, meditation and intercession and not quoted by rote. The first request within Jesus' model of prayer was, "Hallowed be Your name." (Matt. 6:9) After God drew Moses to the burning bush to send him to be the deliverer of the Children of Israel, Moses expressed several concerns. One concern was that when he told the Israelites that the God of their fathers had sent him to them, they would ask, "What is His name?" So Moses asked God, "Then what shall I tell them?" God responded, "I AM WHO I AM. This is what you are to say to the Israelites: 'I AM has sent me to you.'" (Ex. 3:13,14) Yahweh is the Hebrew translation for I AM. God then told Moses that from generation to generation He would be known by that name. It is the name of Yahweh, which God gave Moses, that I believe Jesus was praying in the Lord's Prayer when He prayed, "Hallowed be Your name."

The Eleven Names of Yahweh

In the Old Testament there are eleven compound names [1] of Yahweh. Yahweh means the Self-Existing One. Each compound name of Yahweh emphasizes an aspect of God's character. On specific occasions when the leaders of the Children of Israel found themselves in a place of need, they had an encounter with Yahweh and He met their need. These men of God then described a quality of God's character and in this way many of the compound names of Yahweh are revealed:

- After God provided a ram for Abraham as a substitute for his son, Isaac, Abraham called God **Yahweh-jireh, The LORD Who Provides.**

- When Moses lifted his hands in the wilderness, Joshua and the Children of Israel prevailed in the battle to defeat the Amalekites, Moses gave God the name, **Yahweh-nissi, The LORD Our Banner** on that day.

- When God met with Gideon and set him apart as a mighty warrior to fight the Midians, Gideon was amazed that he saw God and was not killed, so he called God **Yahweh-shalom, The LORD Who Is Peace.**

- Yahweh-sabaot, is first introduced in the writings of Samuel, the prophet. David's declaration to Goliath captures the essence of Yahweh-sabaot, "You come against me with sword and spear and javelin, but I come against you in the name of **Yahweh-sabaot, The LORD Almighty** of the armies of Israel, whom you have defied."

- After David pondered his relationship as a shepherd to his sheep, he realized that was exactly the relationship God had with him and so he declared that God is **Yahweh-rohi, The LORD My Shepherd.**

- When Ezekiel,the prophet, was led into a valley of dry bones, God commanded the prophet to prophesy to the dry bones. Ezekiel declared the name of God and said, "This is what **Yahweh-adonai, the Sovereign LORD** says: Come from the four winds, O breath, and breathe into these slain, that they may live."

There were other specific occasions when the Lord Himself revealed His name to the nation of Israel:

- God promised healing to the children of Israel in the Levitical Law. If they listen to Him and keep His commands, He would not bring on them any diseases He brought upon the Egyptians. God explains that it is because, "I am **Yahweh-rophe, The LORD Who Heals.**

- Again in the Law of Moses, God exhorted the children of Israel to keep and follow His Law. The Lord's declaration of Himself is, "I am **Yahweh-m'kaddesh, The LORD Who Makes Holy."**

- As God spoke of the redemption of Israel, His unfaithful bride, He promises, "With everlasting kindness He will have compassion on you," says **Yahweh-goel, The LORD Your Redeemer.**

- As the Lord reproved the shepherds of Israel for destroying and scattering the sheep of His pasture, He promised He would gather the remnant of His flock and bring them back to their pasture. He would raise up new shepherds and one day He would raise up a righteous branch, who will be a king. This king would be called: **Yahweh-tsidkenu, The LORD Our Righteousness.**

- As the prophet Ezekiel described the dimensions of the New Jerusalem, he said it would be called **Yahweh-shammah, The LORD Who Is There,** because the presence of God would be within its' gates.

The Old and New Testament Pictures of Abiding

The Old Testament picture of asking Yahweh to set His name apart, "Hallowed be Your name", is found in Moses' encounter with God at the burning bush. As Yahweh meets with Moses, He tells Moses that He is sending him to Pharaoh to bring His people, the Israelites, out of Egypt. Moses responds in unbelief and questions what Yahweh is proposing to do by asking, "Who am I?"

Why did Moses respond in this way? The answer is found in the last words the Scriptures record that Moses heard before he left Egypt. Forty years earlier, when Moses was a prince of Egypt, he began to identify with his fellow Israelites. Moses saw one of the Israelites being mistreated by an Egyptian, so Moses went to his defense and avenged him by killing the Egyptian. Moses thought the Hebrews would realize that God was using him to deliver them. The next day Moses saw two Hebrews fighting. When he tried to reconcile them, the one who was mistreating the other pushed Moses aside and said, "Who made you ruler and judge over us?" The man then exposed Moses as the one who killed the Egyptian the day before. Having been exposed as the murderer of the Egyptian, Moses fled to Midian.

"Who made you ruler and judge over us?" were the last words the Scriptures record that Moses heard. In these words Moses' hopes of being a deliverer to the Hebrew people were dashed to pieces. They were words of rejection and they wounded him deeply.

For forty years, Moses, a man who was educated in all the wisdom of the Egyptians and was powerful in speech and action, lived in failure tending sheep. Throughout this period, the memory of the Israelite's words haunted him, "Who made you ruler and judge over us?" "Who made you ruler and judge over us?" "Who made you ruler and judge over us?" So when Yahweh met with him at the burning bush and told Moses that He was sending him to deliver His people, Moses was filled with a great sense of inadequacy. He said, "Who am I, that I should go to Pharaoh and bring the Israelites out of Egypt?" Moses was beaten down, feeling over--whelmed with failure and having no self confidence. God's response to His servant is remarkable, "I will be with you." This simple little statement is the verb form of Yahweh or I Am. It is as though God is saying, "Moses, I am the Self-Existing One! I will be your all in all! I will give you success! You will be the deliverer of My people, because "I Am" is with you!"

When believers pray, "Hallowed be Your name," they are telling Yahweh that they cannot accomplish the task He has called them to do alone. They are asking Yahweh to manifest His nature and power as the I Am, Self-Existing One, to accomplish the task He has called them to do in and through them.

The New Testament picture of coming to the burning bush is found in Hebrews 4:16, "Let us then approach the throne of grace with confidence, so that we may receive mercy and find grace to help us in our time of need." It is a picture of believers drawing near to the Lord Jesus, their great High Priest, in His exalted position at the right hand of the Father to find grace and mercy. When believers draw near to the throne of grace they are saying: "Lord Jesus, we need You." They are appropriating all the present ministry of their great High Priest, the Lord Jesus, in the heavenly realms.

In response to the accusations and questions of the Jews, Jesus said, "Before Abraham was born, I AM!" Jesus makes the claim that He is Yahweh in His response. He fulfills all of the character of God that is revealed in each of the names of Yahweh in His present ministry at the right hand of the Father. When Jesus invited His disciples to abide in Him, He is looking forward to them being seated with Himself in the heavenly places in loving obedience. The process of coming to a place of abiding is appropriating the present work of Jesus in the life of a believer. As believers begin to pray through the Lord's Prayer and make the request, "Hallowed be Your name," they are appropriating the present ministry of Jesus on the throne of grace. In this request, Jesus is suggesting that His disciples appropriate the person and work of Yahweh to meet them in their place of need, so that in the place of abiding they may bear fruit and intercede for the Kingdom of God.

Every day believers make choices by asking themselves:

- Will I try to solve my own problems and/or the needs of others in my own strength?

-- or --

- Will I draw near to the throne of grace and seek the resources of the living Lord Jesus to meet the needs of the day?

The exhortation of Isaiah to the children of Israel was to repent and rest, to be quiet and trust. In so doing, they would find salvation and strength. However, the Hebrew people wouldn't turn to the LORD. And so they were left alone to their own devices. Yet Yahweh was always waiting for them to cry out to Him for help. He longed to be gracious to them and He was waiting to rise and show them compassion. In Isaiah 30:15-18 it reads, "This is what the Sovereign LORD, the Holy One of Israel, says: "In repentance and rest is your salvation, in quietness and trust is your strength, but you would have none of it. You said,'No, we will flee on horses.' Therefore you will flee! You said, 'We will ride off on swift horses.' Therefore your pursuers will be swift! A thousand will flee at the threat of one; at the threat of five you will all flee away, till you are left like a flag staff on a mountaintop, like a banner on a hill." Yet the LORD longs to be gracious to you; He rises to show you compassion. For the LORD is a God of justice. Blessed are all who wait for Him!"

This is the disposition of Jesus, the great High Priest of believers, as He sits on His throne. Jesus sits on a throne of grace. Jesus is longing to be gracious to His followers. Jesus wants to rise from His seat and show them compassion. The problem is believers don't seek Him. They try to meet the challenges of the day in their own strength and they experience something less than the supernatural resources of God revealed in the Scriptures.

In putting these pictures of Moses before the burning bush and Jesus on the throne of grace together it becomes apparent that all the resources of God are available to New Testament believers. When they pray, "Hallowed be Your name" or "Set Yourself apart as Yahweh", believers are coming to a place of abiding. They are acknowledging their inadequacy to accomplish the will of God and intercede on behalf of others. As believers come to a place of abiding, they are asking the Lord Jesus to set Himself apart as Yahweh in their lives. They are appropriating all the resources of the person and work of Christ, particularly His present ministry in the heavenly realms. They are taking hold of every spiritual blessing that is theirs in Christ.

Coming to a place of abiding is a pursuit of intimacy with Jesus. As believers enter into this love relationship with Jesus, they allow the Holy Spirit to convict them of their sin and respond in confession, repentance and obedience to the Lord.[2] They appropriate by faith the person and work of Jesus and, by the ministry of the Holy Spirit, enter into the reality of every spiritual blessing that is theirs in Christ. They affirm [3] the work Jesus has given them to do and the things He is placing in their hands. They allow Jesus to live His life in and through them through the ministry of the Holy Spirit. In this place of abiding, believers listen for what Jesus is doing and they ask accordingly. In this place of abiding, they gain a position of authority in the heavenly realms and intercede for His Kingdom and the needs of others.

You will find eleven written prayers in this booklet that appropriate the compound names of Yahweh. These prayers are intended to be instructive and a model[4] for approaching the throne of grace and coming to a place of abiding in Christ. There is nothing supernatural about them. They are not a formula for "vain repetition". Their purpose is to assist believers in understanding the person and work of Christ and how they might appropriate all the resources of the risen and exalted Lord Jesus in His present ministry.[5] In the front of this booklet on page 6, there is a prayer guide that gives direction on how to appropriate the present ministry of Jesus for a variety of situations that believers and their loved ones may encounter. Many have found the Yahweh Prayer Guide to be a helpful tool in assisting them in discerning what Yahweh prayers to pray as they face the challenges of life.

It has been surprising how the Lord has met with believers as they have used these prayers within small group prayer gatherings. Each member of the group verbally reads a paragraph in rotation. As he/ she reads from their heart and allows the Spirit to lead, the one reading may break out in a song or intercession and then return to the prayer. When the last paragraph is read, the entire group uses the theme of that prayer as a springboard of intercession. They then move on to the next Yahweh prayer, as the Spirit leads.

As you regularly draw near to the Lord Jesus in prayer, it is my hope that:

- In loving Him and responding to Him in obedience, you will be surprised by His presence,

- In declaring the truth of the person and work of Christ, by the power of the Holy Spirit, you will find new courage and faith to serve Him and intercede for others,

- In listening for what Jesus is saying, you will find new insight in praying the will of God on behalf of the Kingdom and others, and

- In abiding in Him, you will watch the Lord Jesus answer your prayers in supernatural ways to the glory of His name.

Jesus is waiting at the edge of His throne of grace to respond to your need, in order that you may receive mercy and find grace to help in your time of need. What is your struggle today?

- Are you filled with guilt and shame and feel disqualified to enter into the presence of a holy God as a result? Jesus is the Righteous One and your defender! He longs to be gracious to you!

- Are you in bondage to sin and cannot get free? Jesus is the Lamb of God who takes away the sins of the world! He rises to have compassion on you!

- Are you experiencing hardships in your life? Jesus is the author and perfecter of faith! He longs to be gracious to you!

- Are you longing for the presence of God? Jesus is the Head of the church and He has prepared a place for you! He rises to show compassion to you!

- Are you anxious and fearful? Jesus is a High Priest after the order of Melchizedek, King of Salem, King of Peace! He longs to be gracious to you!

- Are you ill or injured? It is in the name of Jesus that the sick are healed and the demons are bound. He rises to show you compassion!

- Are you in need of provision? It is according to the Father's riches in Christ that He has promised to supply all of your needs! He longs to be gracious to you!

- Are you in need of care and guidance? Jesus is the Good Shepherd and the Shepherd of your soul! He rises to show compassion to you!

- Are there loved ones around you who are struggling in their Christian lives? Jesus ever lives to make intercession! He longs to be gracious to you!

- Are you struggling to fulfill the ministry the Lord Jesus has called you to? Jesus is building His church! He will give you heavenly resources to accomplish the work He has called you to do. He rises to show you compassion!

- Are you experiencing spiritual attacks from the enemy? Jesus is the Son of God and He sends His angels to war on your behalf! He longs to be gracious!

Choose life today! Come to the place of abiding/oneness with Jesus at the throne of grace by appropriating His present ministry through the prayers of Yahweh.

The Names of Yahweh & The Present Ministry of Jesus

Come to the place of abiding by appropriating the present ministry of Jesus in the heavenly realms. Picture yourself as Moses before the LORD, Yahweh, at the burning bush. The LORD is sending you to touch a needy world. Approach the throne of grace that you may find mercy and grace in this moment of prayer. Appropriate the truths found in the compound names of Yahweh and the present ministry of Jesus that will make you competent to draw near to the Father, intercede for the Kingdom and accomplish His calling in your life (Ex 3:1-15 & Heb 4:14-16).

Yahweh-tsidkenu

Jer 23:5,6   The LORD Our Righteousness

1 John 2:1,2   The Righteous One who speaks in our defense

Yahweh-goel

Is 54:5-8   The LORD Your Redeemer

Rev 5:6-10   The lamb of God

Yahweh-m'kaddesh

Lev 20:8   The LORD Who Makes Holy

Heb 12:2   The author and perfecter of our faith

Yahweh-shammah

Eze 48:35   The LORD Who Is There

Eph 1:22   The head of the church

Yahweh-shalom

| Jdg 6:24 | The LORD Who Is Peace |
| Heb 7:2 | A High Priest after the order of Melchizedek, King of Salem, The King of Peace |

Yahweh-rophe

| Ex 15:26 | The LORD Who Heals |
| Acts 3:16 | In the name of Jesus, the sick are healed |

Yahweh-jireh

| Gen 22:14 | The LORD Who Provides |
| Phil 4:19 | Through Christ we receive glorious riches |

Yahweh-rohi

| Ps 23 | The LORD my Shepherd |
| 1 Pet 2:25 | The shepherd of my soul |

Yahweh-adonai

| Ez 37:1-9 | The Sovereign LORD |
| Mat 16:16-18 | The builder of the church |

Yahweh-sabaot

| 1Sam 17:47 | The LORD Almighty |
| Heb 1:14 | The Son of Man, who sends His angels |

Yahweh-nissi

| Ex 17:8-15 | The LORD Our Banner |
| Heb 7:23-28 | A High Priest after the order of Melchizedek, who lives to make intercession |

The Prayers of Yahweh

Yahweh-tsidkenu, (tsid k' nu)

The LORD Our Righteousness

As the Lord reproves the shepherds of Israel for destroying and scattering the sheep of His pasture, He promises He will gather the remnant of His flock and bring them back to their pasture. He will raise up new shepherds. One day He will raise up a righteous branch, who will be a king. This king will be called, Yahweh-tsidkenu, The LORD Our Righteousness. The following prayer appropriates the name of Yahweh-tsidkenu and the present ministry of Jesus, the Righteous One, as our advocate before the Father for those who are filled with guilt and/or shame.

Who am I? Lord Jesus, You are Yahweh-tsidkenu, the LORD Our Righteousness! As I come to You in this time of prayer I am overwhelmed with my sin. I am grateful for the truth that, as I approach Your throne of grace in this moment, You do not condemn me but are able to sympathize with my weaknesses.

Lord Jesus, in Your life You were tempted in all points as I am; yet You were without sin. In Your death, You who knew no sin became sin on my behalf that I might know the righteousness of God. You became the propitiation for my sins and satisfied the wrath of God on the cross. Because You did a perfect work of justification on the cross, You were raised from the dead.

Now, at the right hand of the Father, You are the Righteous One and You are my advocate with the Father defending me day and night against the accusations of the devil.

Who am I that I should come into the presence of a holy God? Lord Jesus, set Yourself apart as the LORD Our Righteousness. Lord Jesus, I am in need of Your forgiveness and cleansing. I confess to You my sins of _____. Oh, how my sins must grieve You. Yet it was for these very acts that You died on the cross. Cleanse me and wash me from my sins! In Your name I ask, forgive me for my sins! *(Pause for a moment and let the Lord Jesus restore you & cleanse you. Receive His forgiveness.)* Thank You for Your faithfulness. Thank You for Your righteousness. Thank You for Your cleansing. Thank You for Your forgiveness. I am grateful that You do truly sympathize with my weaknesses.

Lord Jesus, I do not want to put any confidence in my flesh to live a righteous life before You in this moment. Whatever has been gained by me through acts of righteousness done in the past I now count as loss that I might gain You. I want to be found in You, not having a righteousness of my own that is from the law, but that which is from You and is by faith. Lord Jesus, You are the LORD Our Righteousness! Set Yourself apart as Yahweh-tsidkenu, the LORD Our Righteousness. In Your name! Amen.

Yahweh-goel, (go el')
The LORD Your Redeemer

As God speaks of the redemption of Israel, His unfaithful bride, He promises, "With everlasting kindness he will have compassion on you," says Yahweh-goel, the LORD Your Redeemer. The following is a prayer appropriating the name of Yahweh-goel, the LORD Your Redeemer and the present ministry of Jesus as the Lamb of God seated on the throne for someone who needs freedom from sin.

1. *Out of the depths I cry to You, O LORD;*
2. *O Lord, hear my voice. Let Your ears be attentive to my cry for mercy.*
3. *If You, O LORD, kept a record of sins, O Lord, who could stand?*
4. *But with You there is forgiveness; therefore You are feared.*
5. *I wait for the LORD, my soul waits, and in His word I put my hope.*
6. *My soul waits for the Lord more than watchmen wait for the morning, more than watchmen wait for the morning.*
7. *O Israel, put your hope in the LORD, for with the LORD is unfailing love and with Him is full redemption.*
8. *He Himself will redeem Israel from all their sins. Psalm 130*

Who am I? Lord Jesus, You are Yahweh-goel, the LORD Your Redeemer. You are the Lamb who was slain and is now seated upon the throne. In Your name, set Yourself apart as Yahweh-goel, the LORD Your Redeemer in my life.

Lord Jesus, You are the Lamb of God who takes away the sins of the world. You were led as a lamb to the slaughter. The Lord has laid on You the iniquity of us all. You are the Passover Lamb who has been sacrificed, and we have been redeemed with Your precious blood. You were raised, and now You are the Lamb who was slain, seated on the throne. With Your blood You have purchased men and women for God from every tribe and language and people and nation. You have made them to be kings and priests to serve our God, and they will reign on the earth. Worthy is the Lamb who was slain to receive power and wealth and wisdom and strength and honor and glory and praise.

Who am I that I should free myself from the power of sin? Set Yourself apart as Yahweh-goel, the LORD Your Redeemer! In Your name Lord Jesus, redeem me from my sins. Have mercy on me, Lamb of God, have mercy. I confess my sins of _____
and _____ to You, Lamb of God. *(Patiently wait for the Holy Spirit to convict you of your sin.)* Have mercy on me, Lamb of God, have mercy. Wash me and I will be white as snow. Cleanse me and I will be like wool *(Wait patiently for a sense of hope from the cleansing of the Lamb)*.

Thank You for the riches of Your grace. Thank You for the redemption that is in You, my Christ. Thank You for redeeming me from my empty way of life. With deep compassion bring me back to You, Lord Jesus. With everlasting kindness have compassion on me and redeem me from my sins, Lamb of God. Set me free from the bondage of these sins that have overtaken me. By Your blood, Lamb of God, I have overcome the devil. Let me overcome in these areas of sin in my life. Let me know Your redemption from my sins that I may serve You as a priest and reign with You as a king. In Your name, set Yourself apart as Yahweh-goel, the LORD Your Redeemer, Lamb of God. Amen.

Yahweh-m'kaddesh, (ma ka dish')
The LORD Who Makes Holy

In the Law of Moses, God exhorts the children of Israel to keep and follow His Law. The Lord's declaration of Himself is, "I am Yahweh-m'kaddesh, the LORD Who Makes Holy." The following is a prayer appropriating the name of Yahweh-m'kaddesh, the LORD Who Makes Holy and the present work of Jesus as the author and perfecter of our faith in the life of a believer who is experiencing hardships.

Who am I? Lord Jesus, You are the LORD Who Makes Holy, Yahweh-m'kaddesh. You are the author and the perfecter of my faith. I thank You for the hardships of life. I affirm that it is Your love that motivates You in chastening me. I affirm that Your purpose in this trial is that I may share in Your holiness and that a harvest of righteousness and peace might be yielded in my life.

Lord Jesus, in Your life You sanctified Yourself that Your followers might be sanctified. You became sanctification on the cross. You learned obedience in the things You suffered and were made perfect through suffering. Through Your death I am dead to sin and through Your resurrection I am alive to You so that sin should no longer reign in my body. Now, You reign at the right hand of the Father and You are the author and perfecter of my faith.

Who am I that I should make my household or myself holy? Lord Jesus, set Yourself apart as the LORD Who Makes Holy. Protect my household from the evil one. In the authority of Your name and by the power of Your blood,[1] I rebuke[2] every scheme and every work of the evil one to make _____ *(List your family members, yourself and the people the Lord Jesus is entrusting to you by name.)* fall short of the grace of God through a bitter spirit, immorality or godlessness. I ask that this hardship of _____ that we are enduring be of Your hand and Your hand alone. In Your name, Lord Jesus, accomplish Your purpose in this trial that we may share in Your holiness. Yield a harvest of righteousness and peace in our lives through this hardship. As we study Your Word today, sanctify us in Your truth. In Your name!

Lord Jesus, I choose to look away from everything else unto You. I look away from these hardships I am enduring and look to You. I choose to meditate on the way You endured the suffering of the cross and hardships at the hands of sinful men. You are the author of my faith. You are the perfecter of my faith. In Your name, Lord Jesus, set Yourself apart as the LORD Who Makes Holy, Yahweh-m'kaddesh, in my life and my household this day. Amen.

Yahweh-shammah, (sham mah')
The LORD Who Is There

As the prophet Ezekiel describes the dimensions of the New Jerusalem, he said it will be called Yahweh-shammah, the LORD Who Is There, because the presence of God will be within its' gates. The following prayer appropriates the name of Yahweh-shammah, the LORD Who Is There and the present ministry of Jesus as the head of the church seated at the right hand of the Father, so that the believer may experience the presence of Jesus and his position in Christ as a member of Jesus' body seated in the heavenly realms.

Who am I? Lord Jesus, You are the LORD Who Is There, Yahweh-shammah. You are the head of the church and I, as a member of the body of Christ, am seated with You in the heavenly realms.

You are Emanuel, God with us. You are the Word who became flesh and dwelt among us. God was in You reconciling the world to Himself. You were raised from the dead and appeared to the twelve. Now You are seated at the right hand of the Father far above all rulers, powers, authorities and dominions. You are the Head of the church, which is Your body. Lord Jesus, You promised, "If I go and prepare a place for you, I will come back and take you to be with Me that you also may be where I am." You have made me alive in Christ. You have raised me. You have seated me with You in the heavenly realms. Again, You promised, "On that day you will realize that I am in My Father, and you are in Me and I am in you." I am in Christ and Jesus is living in me.

You prayed, "Father I want them to be where I am that they may behold My glory." You sent another counselor, the indwelling Spirit of Truth. He lives in me. He teaches me all things and reminds me of everything You said. He testifies about You. He convicts the world of guilt in regard to sin and righteousness and judgment. He guides me into all truth. He tells me what is yet to come. He brings glory to the Father by taking from what is Yours and making it known to me.

Who am I that I should try to manufacture the presence of the living God? Lord Jesus, I ask for the ministry of the Holy Spirit to strengthen _____ *(Name each member of your household, yourself, and/or the people the Lord Jesus is entrusting to you who may be discouraged.)* with power in our inner person, so that You may dwell in our hearts by faith. I ask that, being rooted and established in Your love, we may have power to understand how wide and long and high and deep Your love is and to know Your love by experience, so that we may be filled to the measure of all the fullness of God.

I ask, Lord Jesus, for the ministry of the Holy Spirit to give wisdom and revelation to _____ *(Name each member of your household, yourself, and the people the Lord Jesus is entrusting to you.)* so that we may know You better. Enlighten the eyes of our hearts, so that we may know the hope to which You have called us, the riches of Your glorious inheritance in us and Your incomparably great power towards us who believe. Surprise us with Your presence throughout this day.

Holy Spirit, remind me of the things Jesus taught. Glorify the Son by making known to me the things that belong to Him. Lord Jesus, as I abide in You and You abide in me, live Your life in me and through me today. Set Yourself apart as the LORD Who Is There, Yahweh-shammah. In Your name I pray. Amen.

Yahweh-shalom, (sha lom')
The LORD Who Is Peace

When God met with Gideon and set him apart as a mighty warrior to fight the Midians, Gideon was amazed that he saw God and was not killed, so he called God Yahweh-shalom, the LORD Who Is Peace. The following prayer is an appropriation of the name of Yahweh-shalom and the present ministry of Jesus as our High Priest after the order of Melchizedek, King of Salem, and King of Peace to bring peace to those who are anxious.

Who am I? Dear Lord Jesus, You are Yahweh-shalom, the LORD Who Is Peace! Gideon was filled with fear when he realized that he had seen the angel of the Lord face to face. But You commanded him to be at peace and not to be afraid. He then gave You the name Yahweh-shalom, the Lord Who Is Peace.

Lord Jesus, You are the Prince of Peace. As the angels praised God in the presence of the shepherds, they announced, *"Peace on earth."* In Your death the Father was reconciling all things to Himself, making peace through Your death. In Your crucifixion, You became our peace, reconciling Jew and Gentile into one body through the cross. When You stood before Your disciples as the resurrected Lord You said twice, *"Peace be with you."* Now You are seated at the right hand of the Father as my High Priest after the order of Melchizedek, the King of Salem, which means King of Peace.

I am grateful that I have peace with You, having been justified by faith. I thank You for the hardships of life, knowing that You are the author and perfecter of my faith. I take comfort in knowing that Your chastening work in my life is motivated by Your love and that You will yield a harvest of righteousness and peace within my life. I am grateful for Your presence that is abiding with me in this moment, that I might experience Your perfect peace. Thank You for Your promise that as I am anxious for nothing but in everything by prayer and supplication make my request known to You with thanksgiving, that the peace of God which surpasses all understanding will guard my heart and my mind.

Who am I that I should cope with the needs I am facing? Lord Jesus, set Yourself apart as the LORD Who Is Peace. I thank You for the pressing needs of today. I seek Your resources for the needs of my family, my church and myself. I give to You _____
(Present to Jesus the people and situations that are burdening you.) I ask, in Your name, that You will _____. *(Call on the promises of God to meet these needs that are burdening your heart.)* Guard my heart and mind with Your shalom that surpasses all understanding, in Jesus' name. I am choosing to let the peace of Christ reign in my heart today. You are the LORD who is peace! In Your name, Lord Jesus, set Yourself apart as Yahweh-shalom, the LORD Who Is Peace in my life today! Amen.

Yahweh-rophe, (ro' phay)
The LORD Who Heals

God promises healing to the Children of Israel in the Levitical Law. If they listen to Him and keep His commands, He will not bring on them any diseases He brought upon the Egyptians. God explains that it is because, "I am Yahweh-rophe, the LORD Who Heals". It is in Jesus' name and the faith that comes through Him that people are healed. The following is a prayer appropriating the name of Yahweh-rophe, the LORD Who Heals and the authority of the name of Jesus to heal those who are sick, diseased or injured.

Who am I? Lord Jesus, You are Yahweh-rophe, the LORD Who Heals! I come to You, seeking Your grace and mercy to heal those who are wounded and ill. I am so grateful that I can draw near to You and call upon Your authority and power to heal these dear ones.

Lord Jesus, the Spirit anointed You to set the captives free, mend the broken hearted, cause the blind to have sight and release the oppressed. In Your life, You took up our infirmities and carried our diseases. When John's disciples asked You if You were the one John spoke of, You responded, "The blind receive sight, the lame walk, those who have leprosy are cured, the deaf hear, the dead are raised." You gave authority to the twelve and then the seventy-two to cast out evil spirits and heal the sick. By Your wounds on the cross we are healed. When You were raised from the dead, the greatest healing of all time took place.

Now You are seated at the right hand of the Father and You have been given a name that is above every name, that at Your name every knee shall bow and every tongue shall confess that You are Lord. Peter healed a man crippled from birth in the name of Jesus. It was Your name, Jesus and the faith that comes through You that gave complete healing to him.

Who am I that I should presume that I could heal someone? Lord Jesus, set Yourself apart as the LORD Who Heals, Yahweh-rophe. As Elijah sought You earnestly and persistently that it might rain; I too come, believing that You are able to heal. You responded with compassion for the sick. I now seek Your mercy and grace on behalf of _____. In Your name, Lord Jesus, that name that is above every name, I rebuke every scheme and work of the evil one to afflict _____ with this _____ *(State the illness, condition or need for inner healing.)* Lord Jesus, I ask that You would take up their infirmity and carry their disease. I ask in Your exalted name, Lord Jesus, that You heal _____'s _____ *(State the person and that part of their spirit, body or soul that is afflicted.)*

Lord, I ask that You give me wisdom to know if it is time to call for the Elders to pray and to lay hands on and pray a prayer of faith in Your name. Set Yourself apart as Yahweh-rophe, the LORD Who Heals, in Your name, Lord Jesus! Amen.

Yahweh-jireh, (ji' ra)
The LORD Who Provides

After God provided a ram for Abraham so that he did not have to sacrifice his son, Isaac, Abraham called God Yahweh-jireh, the LORD Who Provides. The following prayer appropriates the name of Yahweh-jireh, the LORD Who Provides and the Father's promise to supply all of our needs according to His glorious riches in Christ Jesus.

Who am I? You are Yahweh-jireh, the LORD Who Provides. Lord Jesus, it is according to His glorious riches in You that the Father supplies all of my needs.

The birds have nests, the foxes have holes but the Son of Man had no place to lay His head. Yet You led a band of followers and all their needs were provided. Women traveled with You and supported Your needs. You even had a fund for the poor. You fed the five thousand with five loaves and two fish. You fed the four thousand with seven loaves and few small fish. Peter paid taxes with a coin caught in a fish. The disciples fished all night with no catch. You said cast your nets on the other side and their nets were full, to the point of breaking.

You were God's provision of salvation through Your death on the cross. You were raised and now the Father supplies all of my needs according to His glorious riches in You.

Lord Jesus, I ask You to fulfill the promise of Your Word, to throw open the floodgates of heaven and pour out so much blessing that I will not have room enough for it because I tithe to You. Fulfill the promise of Your Word to rebuke the devourer, in Your name, Lord Jesus! In that realm where I am seated with You and the powers of darkness hear Your voice, I ask You to rebuke the devourer in this moment. *(Pause for a moment in reverence, as the Lord Jesus rebukes the devourer.)* They may curse, but You will bless. In Your name, I ask for Your blessing upon my family. I ask that all grace will abound to me and my household today, so that in all things and at all times all our needs will be met. Supply all of our needs according to the Father's glorious riches in You, so that we may abound in every good work You are calling us to do. I ask for _____ _____ *(Specifically ask the Lord for what you are desiring Him to provide for you and the people the Lord Jesus is entrusting to you.)* Who am I that I should provide for all of my needs and abound in every good work You have called me to do? In Your name, Lord Jesus, set Yourself apart as Yahweh-jireh, the LORD Who Provides and supply all of my needs according to Your glorious riches in the heavenly places. Amen.

Yahweh-rohi, (ro e')
The LORD My Shepherd

After David pondered his relationship as a shepherd to his sheep, he realized that was exactly the relationship God had with him and so he declares that God is Yahweh-rohi, the LORD Is My Shepherd. The following is a prayer appropriating the name of Yahweh-rohi, the LORD Is My Shepherd and the present ministry of Jesus as the Chief Shepherd and the Shepherd of our soul in the life of the believer.

1. *The LORD is my shepherd, I shall not be in want.*

2. *He make me lie down in green pastures, He leads me beside quiet waters,*

3. *He restores my soul. He guides me in paths of righteousness for His name's sake.*

4. *Even though I walk through the valley of the shadow of death, I will fear no evil, for You are with me; Your rod and Your staff, they comfort me.*

5. *You prepare a table before me in the presence of my enemies. You anoint my head with oil; my cup overflows.*

6. *Surely goodness and love will follow me all the days of my life, and I will dwell in the house of the LORD forever. Psalm 23*

Who am I? You are Yahweh-rohi, the LORD Is My Shepherd. Lord Jesus, You are the Chief Shepherd and the Shepherd of my soul. Set Yourself apart as Yahweh-rohi, the LORD Is My Shepherd in my life.

Lord Jesus, You are the gate; whoever enters through You will be saved. Your sheep will come in and go out through You and find pasture. You lead and the sheep follow You because they know Your voice. The thief comes only to steal and kill and destroy. You came that that we may have life and have it in its fullness. You are the Good Shepherd, and You laid down Your life for the sheep. You are not a hired hand who runs away when the wolf comes. You are the Good Shepherd. You know Your sheep and they know You and You laid down Your life for the sheep. You had authority to lay it down, and You had authority to take it up again. Three days after Your death, You were raised from the dead. Now, Lord Jesus, You are the Chief Shepherd over all the under-shepherds of Your flock and the Shepherd of my soul.

Who am I that I should care for myself? Lord Jesus set Yourself apart as the Shepherd of my soul. I acknowledge that I am a sheep and You are my Shepherd. I am one of those other sheep that You must also bring into the fold. I want to hear Your voice and follow Your leading today. Shepherd of my soul, I need You today! I am tired and weary. Make me lie down in green pastures and lead me beside quiet waters. In Your name, restore my soul. Lord Jesus, I don't know what to do or how to do it. Lead me in paths of righteousness for Your name's sake. As I walk through the valley of death today, make Your presence known to me. Comfort me with Your rod and Your staff. Lord Jesus, I need to see Your goodness and mercy once more. Spread a table before me in the presence of my enemies. Anoint my head with oil. Let my cup overflow, in Your name! I am so grateful for the confidence I have of Your goodness and mercy for me and that I will dwell in Your house forever.

Lord Jesus, You are Yahweh-rohi, the LORD Is My Shepherd. You are the Shepherd of my soul. Lord Jesus, set Yourself apart as the LORD Is My Shepherd in my life and the lives of my loved ones! In Your name I pray. Amen!

Yahweh-adonai, (ad e' ni)
The Sovereign LORD

When Ezekiel, the prophet, was led into a valley of dry bones, God commands the prophet to prophesy to the dry bones. Ezekiel declared the name of God and says, "This is what Yahweh-adonai, the Sovereign LORD says: 'Come from the four winds, O breath, and breathe into these slain, that they may live.'" The following is a prayer appropriating the name of Yahweh-adonai, the Sovereign LORD and the present ministry of Jesus as the builder of His church in the life of a Christian leader.

Who am I? A man can have nothing unless it is given to him from above. Lord Jesus, You are Yahweh-adonai, the Sovereign LORD. You are building Your church and just as the Father sent You, so You are sending me.

Lord Jesus, the Spirit of the Sovereign LORD was upon You. In Your earthly ministry, the Spirit anointed You to preach good news to the poor, to proclaim freedom to the prisoners, to bind up the broken hearted, to give recovery of sight to the blind, and to release from darkness the oppressed.

The Father gave you a work to preach the word of God to the lost sheep of Israel, to train the twelve, to give Your life as a ransom for many and to destroy the works of the devil. You brought glory to the Father by completing the work He gave You. The Father gave You the resources to complete the work. The Father gave you authority that You might give eternal life to all those He had given to You. The Father gave you His words that You might give them to those He entrusted You. You protected those the Father gave You by the power of the name He gave you that they might be one. You gave them the glory that the Father gave You that they might be one. The Father gave You the Spirit without limit. Because He loved You, the Father placed all things in Your hands. All that You had was the Father's and all that the Father had was Yours. None of Your followers had been lost except the one doomed to destruction, so that Scripture would be fulfilled.

You were raised from the dead and when You ascended to heaven, You gave gifts to men. Now You are building Your church. As the Father sent You, You sent Your disciples.

Who am I that I should serve You, the living God? Lord Jesus, set Yourself apart as Yahweh Adonai, the Sovereign LORD. You are building Your church. As the Father sent You, You are sending me. I affirm that You have given me this work of _____ to do. *(Affirm Jesus' calling in your life, quoting the scriptures, praying through the themes of the word pictures or singing the songs he has given to you.)*

I ask in Your name, Lord Jesus that You anoint me with Your Spirit today just as the Father anointed You. Just as the Father loved You and placed all things in Your hands, I affirm that You love me and are giving to me Your authority that I may minister to those You are entrusting to me. I affirm that You are giving me Your words that I may give them to those You are giving to me. You are giving me Your name that I may protect those in prayer that You are entrusting to me. I affirm that You are giving me Your glory that I may give it to them. Lord Jesus, all that I have is Yours and all that You have is mine. I affirm that You are giving _____ to me. *(Affirm the who and what of the people the Lord Jesus is entrusting to you.)*

Build Your church, Lord Jesus! Set Yourself apart as Yahweh-adonai, the Sovereign LORD, in my life. In Your name, I pray! Amen.

Yahweh-nissi, (nis' se)
The LORD Our Banner

When Moses lifted his hands in the wilderness, Joshua and the Children of Israel prevailed in the battle to defeat the Amalekites. Moses gave God the name, Yahweh-nissi, the LORD Our Banner on that day. The following prayer appropriates the name of Yahweh-nissi, the LORD Our Banner and the present ministry Jesus interceding at the right hand of the Father.

Who am I? Lord Jesus, You are Yahweh-nissi, the LORD Our Banner! As Moses lifted up his hands in the wilderness, Joshua and the Children of Israel prevailed in the battle against the Amalekites. When his hands were lowered, the Amalekites prevailed in the battle. Through the support of Aaron and Hur, Moses' hands remained lifted and Israel was victorious on that day.

Lord Jesus, as You were baptized, You prayed and the Father affirmed You as the Son and the Spirit came upon You as a dove. When faced with the seduction of success in Capernaum, as the whole town came to You, You rose very early in the morning and went to a solitary place to pray. You told Your disciples that You had to go to other villages to preach, for that is what You were sent to do. You prayed through the night and then You chose the twelve and appointed them as apostles. Though the news about You spread, so that crowds of people came to hear You and be healed of their sicknesses, You often withdrew to lonely places and prayed. When You fed the five thousand and they tried to make You king, You withdrew and prayed into the evening. Later that night, You walked on water and the next day, You proclaimed that You were the bread of life and were not establishing an earthly kingdom at that time. When the multitudes could not accept Your words and left You, the twelve remained because You had the words of life.

You prayed and Peter was given insight to declare that You were the Christ, the Son of the Living God. You then told them that upon the rock of Peter's confession You would build Your church. You then began to disclose to them that You would go to Jerusalem to suffer at the hands of the religious leaders and be put to death. Nine days later, You prayed and Peter, James and John beheld Your glory on the mount of transfiguration. Satan desired to sift Peter as wheat, but You prayed for him that his faith might not fail, and it didn't. You protected Your disciples in prayer by the name the Father gave You. You prayed in the garden and found the strength to bear the cup of wrath the Father had for You and You made atonement for the sins of the world.

In Your death, You were numbered with the transgressors. You made intercession for transgressors. Now, You are a High Priest after the order of Melchizedek. You are able to save completely because You always live to make intercession for the saints.

Lord Jesus, I am grateful that even in this moment You are praying for me. Holy Spirit, I thank You for revealing Jesus to me and leading me in this time of intercession. I am thankful that You are interceding for me as well. I am comforted by the knowledge that You know my weaknesses and pray with groans in accordance with the Father's will when I don't know how to pray.

Who am I that I should pray for those You have entrusted to me and expect that they would have victory in their lives? Lord Jesus, set Yourself apart as Yahweh-nissi, the LORD Our Banner! Intercede for them in this moment, my High Priest! As I pray for these You have entrusted to me, give them victory in their lives for Your glory and honor. In Your name! Amen.

Yahweh-sabaot, (sa ba' ohth)

the LORD Almighty

Yahweh-sabaot, is first introduced in the writings of Samuel, the prophet. David's declaration to Goliath captures the essence of Yahweh-sabaot, the LORD of Almighty, "You come against me with sword and spear and javelin, but I come against you in the name of Yahweh-sabaot, the LORD Almighty of the armies of Israel, whom you have defied. The following is a prayer appropriating the name of Yahweh-sabaot, the LORD Almighty and the present ministry of Jesus as the Son of God to send His angels to protect the believer and to war against the powers of darkness as the believer advances the Kingdom.

1. *He who dwells in the shelter of the Most High will rest in the shadow of the Almighty.*

2. *I will say of the LORD, "He is my refuge and my fortress, my God, in whom I trust."*

3. *Surely He will save you from the fowler's snare and from the deadly pestilence.*

4. *He will cover you with His feathers, and under His wings you will find refuge; His faithfulness will be your shield and rampart.*

5. *You will not fear the terror of night, nor the arrow that flies by day,*

6. *nor the pestilence that stalks in the darkness, nor the plague that destroys at midday.*

7. *A thousand may fall at your side, ten thousand at your right hand, but it will not come near you.*

8. *You will only observe with your eyes and see the punishment of the wicked.*

9. *If you make the Most High your dwelling—even the LORD, who is my refuge—*

10. *then no harm will befall you, no disaster will come near your tent.*

11. *For He will command His angels concerning you to guard you in all your ways;*

12. *they will lift you up in their hands, so that you will not strike your foot against a stone.*

13. You will tread upon the lion and the cobra;

14. you will trample the great lion and the serpent.

15. *"Because he loves Me," says the LORD, "I will rescue him; I will protect him, for he acknowledges My name.*

16. He will call upon Me, and I will answer him;

17. *I will be with him in trouble, I will deliver him and honor him.*

18. *With long life will I satisfy him and show him My salvation."*
    Psalm 91

Who am I that I should war against the powers of darkness? Lord Jesus, You are Yahweh-sabaot, the LORD Almighty. When David approached Goliath in the battlefield he said, "You come against me with sword and spear and javelin, but I come against you in the name of the LORD Almighty of the armies of Israel, whom you have defied." You are the Son of God, and as the Son, You send Your angels to war on behalf of the saints.

You are the seed of the woman who crushed the head of the serpent. From the time of John the Baptist and throughout Your ministry, the Kingdom of God was advancing by force and You, as a forceful Man, took hold of it. The devil challenged Your role as the Son at the temptation in the wilderness. You never yielded to him and, in resisting the devil, You bound the strong man and throughout Your ministry took the spoils.

You were condemned for being the Son of Man. You could have called on the Father, and He would have put at Your disposal more than twelve legions of angels to rescue You, but You submitted to the Father and went to the cross. The devil bruised Your heel, but You crushed his head on the cross.

You were declared with power to be the Son of God by Your resurrection from the dead. As the Son, You came in order to destroy the works of the devil.

Now You are building Your church and the gates of Hades will not overcome it. You give the keys of the Kingdom of Heaven to men. Whatever they bind on earth is bound in heaven and whatever they loose on earth is loosed in heaven. You send Your angels to war on behalf of the saints.

Who am I that I should enter into this spiritual warfare for the Kingdom of Heaven? Lord Jesus, I have made You my dwelling. I love You and I now call upon Your name. Set Yourself apart as Yahweh-sabaot, the LORD Almighty. As the Son of God, command Your angels to guard _____ *(Name each member of your household, yourself and the people the Lord Jesus is entrusting to you.)* in all of our ways. I pray that no harm will befall us and no disaster will come near our tents.

As I enter into this warfare, empower me by the Holy Spirit to advance Your Kingdom by force. Grant me Your authority that I may, as a forceful person, lay hold of it. Son of God, as I war for Your Kingdom with the powers of darkness, send Your angels to war against every scheme and work of the evil one. I enter into this warfare in the name of Yahweh-sabaot, the LORD Almighty. Lord Jesus, You are the Son of God. Set Yourself apart as Yahweh-sabaot, the LORD Almighty, in my life and in the lives of those I am interceding for in this moment. In Your name! Amen.

NOTES

Introduction

1. Norman Grubb, *Rees Howells Intercessor* (Fort Washington, Pennsylvania: Christian Literature Crusade 1952) 64, 65

2. Andrew Murray, *The Andrew Murray Collection: Abide In Me* (Uhrichsville, Ohio: Barbour and Company, Inc.) 27

3. Norman Grubb, *Rees Howells Intercessor* (Fort Washington, Pennsylvania: Christian Literature Crusade 1952) 63, 64

How do we abide in Christ?

1. D. M. Lloyd Jones, *God's Ultimate Purpose* (Grand Rapids, Michigan, Baker Book House 1979) 350

2. Larry Lea, *Could You Not Tarry For One Hour* (Altamonte Springs, FL: Creation House, 1987) 58, 59

The Eleven Names of Yahweh

1. Larry Lea, *Could You Not Tarry For One Hour* (Altamonte Springs, FL: Creation House, 1987) 60, 63, 64, 69, 73, 74, 75

2. Norman Grubb, *Rees Howells Intercessor* (Fort Washington, Pennsylvania: Christian Literature Crusade 1952) 64

3. Geraldine Taylor, *Behind The Ranges: The Life-changing Story of J.O. Fraser* (Singapore, OMF International Ltd. 1998) 135

4. Mark I. Bubeck, *The Rise of Fallen Angels* (Chicago, IL, Moody Press 1995) 102

5. Mark I. Bubeck, *Overcoming the Adversary* (Chicago, IL, Moody Press 1984) 38-42

Yahweh - m' kaddesh

1. Mark I. Bubeck, Overcoming the Adversary (Chicago, IL, Moody Press 1984) 32

2. Neil T. Anderson, The Bondage Breaker (Eugene, Oregon, Harvest House Publishers 1990) 190

ABOUT THE AUTHOR

Clyde was born and grew up in Southern California. He is a graduate of Biola University and Talbot Theological Seminary. He and his wife, Mary Lynne, were married in June 1976. They have three daughters Kara, Lindsay and Meagan, and are thankful for their growing family through marriage and grandchildren.

Mary Lynne and Clyde's youth pastor, Dave Griener, mentored them to love God's word and hear His voice through the word. Dave taught them to study and memorize God's word, as well as, to pray for hours. Clyde has always been given to prayer because of the grounding he received in those early days of faith in Christ. An intercessory gift began to emerge in 1984, as Clyde experienced frustration with the lack of fruitfulness in ministry. Prayer became a part of everything he did. Clyde has watched the Father fulfill His promises to answer prayer over and over again. Clyde has been equipping the Body of Christ to pray and has led a variety of prayer efforts since 1989.

Clyde served in various associate pastoral positions for twenty-five years and sensed God's call to pray for the nations in November of 2000. He was the Director of Prayer Ministries at MentorLink International through 2008 and then launched PrayerMentor ministry, where he serves as the President. Through these ministries he's led prayer efforts and mentored national pastors in 25 nations through 55 international trips.

Clyde mentors pastors, ministry leaders and business owners in prayer, cares for their souls and builds prayer teams around them so that they may fulfill the work Jesus has given to them, thereby glorifying the Father and advancing the Kingdom of God on earth. In 2011, Clyde and Mary Lynne began intentionally discipling international students and praying in the villages of unreached people groups to bring about Disciple Making Movements among the nations.

A Prayer Mentor Book Series

Coming to a Place of Abiding

Equipping believers to come to a place of abiding by appropriating
the present ministry of Jesus in the heavenly realms through
the Yahweh prayers.

God's Calling

Equipping Christian leaders and intercessors to discern God's calling
in their lives and assert the authority of their calling as forceful men
and women by praying Kingdom prayers through the themes of John

Prayer Efforts

Equipping the body of Christ to persist in prayer through
a variety of prayer efforts in order to gain a position of authority
over the enemy and fulfill the calling of the Lord Jesus in their lives.

Made in the USA
Coppell, TX
10 February 2022

73339592R00039